Churchyards and Cemeteries

KENNETH HUDSON

THE BODLEY HEAD
LONDON SYDNEY
TORONTO

ACKNOWLEDGMENTS

Thanks are due to the following for supplying photographs: Richard Ashdown, front cover; page 3 by permission of the Sutcliffe Gallery, by agreement with Whitby Literary and Philosophical Society; BBC Hulton Picture Library, pages 4, 6, 16, 31 (left and right) and 35 (top); Mary Evans Picture Library, pages 7, 9, 20, 21 and 37; The Museum of London, page 8 (left); pages 10, 24 and 25 (left) © Vera Collingwood, photographs first appeared in *London Cemeteries* (Avebury) by Hugh Meller; Golders Green Crematorium, page 11 (bottom); Liverpool City Libraries, pages 12 and 15 (top); The Grange Museum Collection (London Borough of Brent), page 13; The Mitchell Library, Glasgow, pages 14–15 and 25 (right); Wellington Enterprises, Stratfield Saye, Reading, page 17 (bottom); © Durham University, page 18; The Vicar of St Leonard's Church, Hythe, Kent, page 19; John Gay, pages 22–23 and 46; pages 26–27, reproduced by gracious permission of Her Majesty the Queen; Pamela Burgess, pages 28 and 30; Sussex Archaeological Society, page 29. All other photographs © Ann Nicholls, 1984.

Front cover photograph is of Ditcheat Churchyard, Somerset. Back cover photographs show: stone skeleton from Painswick, Glos.; carved stone tree from Lansdown Cemetery, Bath and a grand tomb from Arno's Vale cemetery, Bristol.

British Library Cataloguing
in Publication Data
Hudson, Kenneth
Churchyards and cemeteries.
1. Cemeteries – Juvenile literature
I. Title
393.1   GT3320
ISBN 0–370–30543–4

Text © Kenneth Hudson 1984
Printed in Great Britain for
The Bodley Head Ltd, 9 Bow Street,
London WC2E 7AL
by William Clowes Ltd, Beccles
Set in 12 on 14 pt Ehrhardt
First published 1984

Contents

The difference between a churchyard
   and a cemetery, 5
The numbers who died, 6
Finding somewhere to bury them, 8
Crematoria, 10
The private cemeteries, 12
Animal graves, 16
Graveyard monuments, 18
The poor and the rich, 20
Burial places of the great, 22
The grand monuments, 24
The graves of the royal family, 26

Headstones, 28

The masons' materials, 29

Inscription spotting, 31

Chest and table tombs, 34

Victorian privacy and respectability, 36

Symbols, 38

Military cemeteries, 42

Burial places as parks, 44

The problems of neglect, 46

Index, 48

The difference between a churchyard and a cemetery

We have churchyards and we have cemeteries and the difference between them is important. English churchyards grew slowly and gradually; a few more graves were added each year until they were full and then room was made for another crop of burials by disturbing the ancient bones which were already there.

Cemeteries are different. Most of them came into existence during the nineteenth century as an attempt to solve one of the problems caused by large numbers of people flooding into the towns and cities to work. These immigrants, hundreds of thousands of them, were born in the country and died in the town, where room had somehow to be found to bury them. The new cemeteries were set up, like the drains and the water supply, to meet an urgent practical need. Some have been well kept and some are vandalised and neglected and a disgrace to a civilized country.

But, whatever their age, size or condition, both churchyards and cemeteries are wonderful places for finding out about our ancestors. I am a cemetery enthusiast, because I know of no better way of absorbing the atmosphere of the past. By browsing among the tombstones you can learn so much – the length of people's lives at different periods, the facts about family size and infant mortality, the effects of wars and epidemics, the range of occupations, the extent to which people moved about the country, and so on. This book suggests some of the things to look for in churchyards and cemeteries that will help you to accumulate this fascinating information about our past.

Don't, by the way, go prowling about inside old tombs. They can easily collapse on top of you. As you can see when you walk around a cemetery that's been established for a long time, some of the monuments and tombs have got into a pretty ruinous condition.

The numbers who died

The first official Census was held in 1801. It showed that the total population of England and Wales in that year was a little under nine million. Before this date, the figures are very unreliable, but it seems likely that the total had been something like seven million in 1700. During the eighteenth century, the growth of the population had therefore been very slow.

But totals tell only part of the story. To get a satisfactory picture of what happened, we need to know why the population changed so little during the eighteenth century and why it grew so fast in the nineteenth. And the answer to that question is complicated. One reason why the number of people in Britain remained almost stationary for the first three-quarters of the eighteenth century was that the death rate was so high. In 1700 it was twenty-six per thousand, that is, twenty-six out of every

'A rare old British worthy is carried to his last home.' An English country funeral in the late eighteenth century

Funeral service, circa 1833

thousand people died each year – the figure today, in 1984, is about eleven – and during the next thirty years the death rate actually passed the birth rate. By 1746 it had reached the remarkable level of thirty-five per thousand. But this figure was for the country as a whole. In some areas, it was as high as fifty.

The good places, where one was rather less likely to die early, were in the country and the bad places were in the larger towns, particularly London. There is no mystery about why this was so. The towns had a poor drainage system and a water supply which was often dangerous to health, so that diseases spread quickly. And the bigger the towns became, as families drifted out of agriculture and into industry, the more people were crammed into each acre and the worse the health problem was. There was no general improvement until the Public Health Acts of the second half of the nineteenth century.

Finding somewhere to bury them

Children suffered most from insanitary conditions and disease. During the first half of the eighteenth century, three-quarters of the children in London died before they were five. By 1850, this proportion had come down to one-third, but throughout the Victorian period, when large families were the rule, most parents, of all classes, had to reckon that one or two of their children would die in infancy. The gravestones make clear what was happening.

There were consequently a great many people to bury. As a rough estimate, one

Infant mortality in the mid nineteenth century

could say that in 1700 there would have been approaching 182,000 funerals of one kind or another each year, compared with approximately 500,000 at the present time. But the difference is not simply one of numbers. In 1700 and throughout the eighteenth century nearly everyone was buried in a churchyard, whereas today most churchyards are full and burials have to take place in big cemeteries provided and run by the local authority. In the past, few churchyards had to deal with more than twenty funerals a year and quite a number only two or three. A modern cemetery is concerned with hundreds.

There is a further complication. In the eighteenth century, and for most of the nineteenth, everyone was buried. Cremation in Britain only became legal in 1884 and for a long time it was considered by most people to be a rather peculiar and not very reverent way of disposing of the dead. Nowadays, however, about two out of every three people are cremated.

Highgate Cemetery, London, established in 1839

9

Crematoria

The Cremation Society was founded in 1874 by Sir Henry Thompson, surgeon to Queen Victoria. An acre of land was bought near Woking Cemetery and the first cremation took place there in 1885. Manchester, Glasgow and Liverpool built crematoria in the 1890s and one for North London, at Golders Green, opened in 1902. Before that, all Londoners who had indicated a wish to be cremated had to be taken to Woking by rail from a private station at Westminster Bridge Road. About fifty a day made this journey.

Golders Green was, and still is, much larger than any other crematorium. It had four gas-fired furnaces, which produced the more than adequate heat of 2000°F, close to the melting point of silver, and by the 1930s it was dealing with a quarter of all the cremations in Britain, about 7,500 a year. Since then, the opening of eighteen more crematoria in the London area has reduced the annual number of cremations at Golders Green to about 3,500.

Even with the steadily increasing popularity of cremation, it has been

Golders Green

Columbarium, Arno's Vale cemetery, Bristol △

Scale of Charges at Golders Green, 1912 ▷

very difficult to find sufficient space for burials. Without cremation, it is dreadful to think what the situation might have been. So much of Britain would have been covered by cemeteries that there would hardly have been room for the living.

Crematoria do not have anything that can be compared with a churchyard or a cemetery. They are usually surrounded by a well-kept garden but there is little in the way of monuments, although caskets of ashes can be placed in rows of small niches in a columbarium or pigeon-house, and memorial tablets may be fixed to walls provided for the purpose.

The private cemeteries

The dreadfully overcrowded conditions in the late eighteenth century city churchyards provided an opportunity for enterprising people to start cemeteries as speculative businesses. By the 1830s there were fourteen such cemeteries in London alone. In some of them the conditions were scandalous. On one site of less than an acre, 14,000 bodies were buried in less than twenty years, some only two feet deep. In order to pack more in, and therefore make more money, bodies were chopped up and partly burnt, and quicklime was used to speed up decomposition. Bones were ground down and sold as manure, lead coffins were removed and disposed of for the value of the metal and wooden coffins were broken up for firewood.

Similar conditions existed abroad. The French were pioneers in tackling the problem in a serious way. In 1804 they forbade any further burials in city churchyards and

Liverpool Necropolis shortly after it was opened in 1825

established the first large European urban cemetery, at the famous Père Lachaise. The Liverpool Necropolis was the first to open in England in 1825 and the Glasgow Necropolis followed not long afterwards, in 1833,

Plan of Kensal Green Cemetery, 1849. The lines in the print show where the paper was creased during the printing of the original newspaper.

the same year in which Kensal Green was opened by the London Cemetery Company.

But Kensal Green, like Glasgow, was expensive. The cheapest graves there cost £1.50, a sum beyond the reach of the average family. The charge could be defended, however. Good architects had been employed to look after the landscaping and design and this had to be paid for. There was soon a demand that public cemeteries should be provided to cater for the poorer classes and in 1850 the Metropolitan Interments Act, the first of a long series of Burial Acts, gave the Board of Health power to establish new cemeteries and to buy existing private cemeteries.

Liverpool Necropolis, 1912. Compare the print on p.12. ▷
Artist's impression of Glasgow Necropolis, circa 1866 ▽

Animal graves

Nowadays it is not easy to get permission to be buried anywhere outside a churchyard or a cemetery. This is mainly for reasons of public health. If you wanted to be buried in your own garden, your relatives would find it difficult to persuade the local authority that it was a good idea, unless it happened to be a very large garden or a park and the site was well away from habitations. But it is always worth trying and really determined people do sometimes get the burial places they want. Curiously enough, no permission is required to bury a domestic animal, although the body of a dog or a pig might well seem to be as much a danger to public health as that of a human being.

Animal cemetery in Kensington Gardens, pre 1920

There are many animal cemeteries in Britain, which is world-famous as a nation of dog and cat lovers. Owners of departed pets often spend large sums on headstones and other forms of monuments. Such pet cemeteries, however, are purely commercial ventures. They have to conform with environmental health legislation, but there is usually no great difficulty over this.

Tombstone erected in 1981 to commemorate Bobby, the faithful Skye terrier who guarded his master's grave in Greyfriars Churchyard, Edinburgh, for 14 years until he himself died.

Tombstone of Wellington's horse, Stratfield Saye, Berks

Graveyard monuments

There are many known examples of prehistoric and Roman burial places in the British Isles and there must be at least as many more which so far remain undiscovered. Nearly all the people involved are anonymous. Apart from a few commemorated by Roman monuments, almost always to the more distinguished and influential people, our forefathers died unrecorded during those centuries.

Later, there are some finely decorated Anglo-Danish tombstones, mostly in the north of England and in Cornwall, and a number of examples of Anglo-Saxon coffin

Viking hogback grave covers from Brompton, Yorkshire

Skulls in crypt, St Leonard's Church, Hythe

slabs or lids. Throughout the Middle Ages, most corpses were wrapped in a shroud, tied head and foot, and the body was then placed straight into the grave, without a coffin. For important people, stone coffins were sometimes used during the twelfth and thirteenth centuries, occasionally with a headstone, but individual churchyard monuments became much less common during the fourteenth century.

The Norman habit, which continued for four centuries after the Conquest and in some places for much longer, was to begin burials on one side of the graveyard site and then work back again, so that there were eventually two or more layers of bones, one on top of the other, in very shallow graves. When even this became difficult, quantities of bones were removed and put into crypts or charnel houses in the adjoining church, so as to make room for more.

In large towns, where overcrowding in graveyards was a particular problem, few families were able to buy plots and so there was little incentive to put up a headstone or any other form of memorial. This situation remained until the cemeteries were established in the nineteenth century.

The poor and the rich

The poor have always died more completely than the rich. For centuries, all the average man and woman and their children received at the end of their life was a hole in the ground, with no sign or monument above ground, except perhaps a simple wooden cross to show where they were buried. Those with money usually did much better. They were able to afford some form of permanent memorial of stone, although 'afford' must in many cases have been a misleading word. 'Somehow found the money for' would often be a more accurate way of describing what happened. Partly for reasons of snobbery, partly as a mark of respect for the dead, families, now as a century ago, will often make great sacrifices in order to have what they would consider a suitable memorial.

Duke of Wellington's funeral, 1852. The hearse, originally housed in the crypt of St Paul's Cathedral, can now be seen in the Wellington Museum at Stratfield Saye, Berks.

To compare prices over a period of two or three hundred years is very difficult and often meaningless but, as a rough guide, one could reckon that the cost of a plain headstone, suitably lettered, has always cost roughly the equivalent of one month's income for someone in the middle of British society. Commemorating the dead has never been cheap, which is one reason why we know quite a lot about people who belonged to the top third of our fellow-citizens and hardly anything, apart from a brief entry in the parish register, about the remaining two-thirds.

An etching, circa 1830

Painswick, in Gloucestershire, was an exceptionally rich town. It owed its prosperity to the woollen industry and the local clothiers and farmers had plenty of money to spend on churchyard monuments. This is why there are so many magnificent tombs and headstones in the churchyard here, to people like 'William Knight, Clothier', 'Richard Smith, Mercer', 'Richard Packer, Woolstapler' and 'John Loveday, Yeoman', and why the town and the surrounding countryside are so full of their fine houses. But, although a thorough excavation of the churchyard would certainly reveal many tons of bones belonging to poor people, there is no indication whatever as to whom they belonged. They have disappeared from history.

Burial places of the great

The great do not necessarily have great monuments, or indeed any monuments at all, but hunting them out can be a special pleasure in a big cemetery. The best way of starting a celebrity chase of this kind is to ask the caretaker of the cemetery to show you the list of burials and grave numbers. Most cemeteries have such a list but, even with its help, the graves may take a lot of finding, especially if the cemetery has become neglected or if the inscriptions are badly worn.

But, as an example of the richness and variety of the discoveries you can make,

here is a very brief selection from among hundreds of equally distinguished people buried at Highgate Cemetery, London: Sir Alfred Barratt (1860–1941), the founder of the famous firm of sweet manufacturers; Dr Jacob Bronowski (1908–74), the scientist and television broadcaster; Charles Cruft (1852–1938), the founder of the dog show; George Eliot (1819–80), the novelist; Michael Faraday (1791–1867), the chemist and electrical pioneer; Richard Smith (1836–1900), who patented the process for making Hovis bread, and Karl Marx (1818–83).

Large city cemeteries in other parts of Britain can also provide excellent hauls of this kind, and you can have a lot of fun building up your own lists.

Karl Marx's tomb, erected 1956 ▷

The grand monuments

From the Middle Ages onwards, many well-to-do and important people have been anxious to have magnificent memorials. Until the early nineteenth century, these memorials were usually placed in churches and cathedrals, but between then and the outbreak of the First World War a great many were put outdoors, in churchyards and cemeteries. There were two reasons for this new custom. One was that there was no room left in the churches, and the other that, as the population grew and the wealth of the country increased, there were a great many more rich and important people to bury and commemorate. The big new cemeteries gave them the opportunity to buy large plots and on these they, or rather their relatives, built great tombs and mausoleums, which often cost as much as the house in which the deceased had lived when alive.

The services of leading sculptors and architects were engaged and large firms of monumental masons were established to carry out the work. The fashionable Victorian cemeteries in London, Edinburgh, Glasgow, Birmingham and other cities are full of examples of huge, elaborate and often, alas, rather vulgar monuments to Victorians and Edwardians with a lot of money and vanity.

At the Necropolis in Glasgow the Monteath mausoleum cost £1,000 in 1851. It

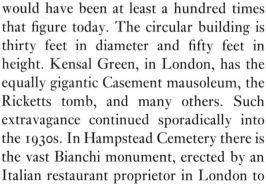

The Monteath mausoleum, circa 1865 △

would have been at least a hundred times that figure today. The circular building is thirty feet in diameter and fifty feet in height. Kensal Green, in London, has the equally gigantic Casement mausoleum, the Ricketts tomb, and many others. Such extravagance continued sporadically into the 1930s. In Hampstead Cemetery there is the vast Bianchi monument, erected by an Italian restaurant proprietor in London to commemorate the death of his wife. Close by is an organist's memorial, in the form of a giant stone organ, complete with music and stool.

Frolics on this scale would no longer be possible in most cemeteries. A Hampstead regulation of 1934 lays down that future memorials should not exceed five feet six inches in height.

The graves of the royal family

Until the end of the eighteenth century, the kings and queens of England were buried in a variety of places. The tombs of Henry VII and James I, for example, are in Westminster Abbey, and that of James II at St Germain-en-Laye, in France. St George's Chapel, Windsor, however, has been the favourite choice. Edward IV and Henry VI are both here and so, too, is Edward VII, in a tomb near the High Altar, guarded by his terrier, Caesar. George III constructed a Royal Vault in the Chapel.

His daughter, Princess Amelia, was the first to be buried there. She was joined in due course by George III, George IV, Queen Charlotte and her two little sons, Alfred and Octavius – they were moved from Westminster – and Edward, Duke of Kent, the father of Queen Victoria. George V followed in his turn. George VI was originally buried here too, but he was moved to a special chapel in 1969.

The Garter Stalls, St George's Chapel, Windsor Castle, circa 1900

The monument of Edward, Duke of Kent, in St George's Chapel, Windsor, circa 1900

Queen Victoria herself went about the task differently. She and her husband, Albert, decided to be buried in a mausoleum specially designed for them at Frogmore, about half a mile from Windsor Castle, across the Royal Park. The Queen's mother, the Duchess of Kent, was the first to be buried in the new mausoleum, in 1861. Prince Albert arrived in 1868, after temporary interment elsewhere, Princess Alice in 1878, Victoria herself in 1901 and Edward VIII in 1972.

Windsor, either in St George's Chapel or at Frogmore, is now the accepted burial place for members of the British royal family.

The royal mausoleum at Frogmore

Headstones

An example of an eighteenth century headstone, Lydney, Glos.

Headstones, the most common form of churchyard memorial, became popular in the sixteenth century, after the Reformation. By the end of the reign of Queen Elizabeth I, the wealth of the country was increasing. Many more people could afford to buy plots and not unnaturally wanted them to be distinguished in some way. The period between 1700 and 1850 produced a great deal of outstanding work from local monumental masons. In some churchyards, one can see from the style of the gravestones that a number of them are the work of the same man. Unfortunately, some of the best craftsmanship was carried out on the softer stones, so that much of the detail has been worn away by weathering.

Some of the early seventeenth century headstones are crudely worked, with uneven and badly spaced lettering. But, in most areas, the eighteenth century brought a considerable improvement, with a wider range of lettering styles and more refinement and variety in the carvings. Some particularly fine work was carried out in slate and, because of the hardness of this material, the beauty of the lettering can still be seen in something close to its original condition.

In one or two areas, such as the South-East, where good workable local stone was not available, wooden graveboards were used, running horizontally along the grave lengthways. They were often painted white and had black lettering. Very few of these have survived, except in museums, but you may occasionally come across something very like them in stone – a curious example of the mason copying the carpenter.

Lettering in Portland stone by Eric Gill, Buckland, Surrey

The masons' materials

Until the coming of the railways, when it became possible for the first time to transport stone cheaply and quickly over long distances, monumental masons used the local stone as a matter of course for most of their work. Only the very rich could afford to have different, better and more prestigious materials brought from outside the district.

But stones vary enormously in their ability to resist the action of rain, wind, frost and old age. The Cotswold limestone –

the one used at Painswick – is a beautiful building stone and it is easy to work and carve, but it wears away fairly quickly, so that many of the inscriptions here are difficult to decipher. The same is true of all the other limestones, including the fashionable and much-used Bath and Portland stone.

This is one reason why local notabilities prefer to have their memorials inside the church, where they were protected against the weather, and where more words commemorating the deceased were possible than on a churchyard monument. And it explains why, over the past one hundred and fifty years, the firms who supply monuments have found it easy to persuade their customers to buy marble or granite which, although usually more expensive, stand up better to the weather.

But, in most churchyards belonging to the Church of England, the use of 'foreign' stones has usually been strictly controlled by the Diocese. It has been the local material or nothing. Cemeteries, on the other hand, have on the whole been more tolerant. We are therefore faced with the unfortunate situation that the older and more interesting stones in churchyards are in poor condition simply because they were made of the local material, which is a great pity.

Footstone of the tomb of Mark Sharp, carpenter,
St John-sub-Castro, Lewes, Sussex

29

(*Overleaf*) ▷
Examples of Victorian lettering used on slate headstones

AGEDSACRE

YEARS ME

ALME HEAR

STAFFORDOF

SACREMORY

EDWARMARSO

ANVRHODA

Inscription spotting

Most churchyards or cemeteries can provide something interesting in the way of inscriptions. It may be a person's curious name, or his occupation, or something connected with his career. Or the fact that she had fifteen children, none of whom lived beyond the age of three. Or that he had some notable invention to his credit.

Sometimes it is a tombstone comment on the deceased which catches the eye. Like this modern one (1968) in the Protestant Cemetery at Corofin in Ireland. It concerns a lady called Audrey Douglas.

'Here as ever sleeping sound,
Lies our Audrey in the ground.
If she wake, as wake she may,
There'll be fun on judgement day.'

Sometimes an inscription will give us some very detailed and intimate information about the deceased. We can read, for instance, at Abney Park, London, about Mary Hillum of Stoke Newington. She lived to be a hundred and five and 'she died in the same house in which she was born, scarcely ever slept out of the house in the whole of her life, never travelled either by

(*Left*) Amusing inscription on the tombstone of an unfortunate soldier, Winchester, Hants

(*Below*) Tomb in Thursley Churchyard, Surrey. Up until the eighteenth century the area was noted for its iron-smelting industry.

IN LOVING MEMORY
OF
GEORGE CRUIKSHANK
ARTIST,
DESIGNER ETCHER PAINTER
BORN SEPT 27TH 1792
DIED FEBY 1ST 1878
AT 263 HAMPSTEAD RD LONDON
AGED 86

FOR 30 YEARS A TOTAL ABSTAINER
AND ARDENT PIONEER AND CHAMP
BY PENCIL WORD AND PEN
OF
UNIVERSAL ABSTINENCE
FROM
INTOXICATING DRINKS

HIS REMAINS
LAID IN THIS CEMETERY
FEBY 9TH 1878
WERE REMOVED ON
NOVR 29TH 1878
TO ST PAUL'S CATHEDRAL
WHERE THEY FINALLY REPOSE

THIS MONUMENT IS ERECTED
BY HIS AFFECTIONATE WIDOW
ELIZA CRUIKSHANK.

△ Kensal Green, London ▷

omnibus or railway and was never more than fifteen miles from home.'

Tombstone inscriptions are a wonderful source of social history. The best collections of occupations on tombstones are to be found in small towns which were prosperous in the eighteenth century and have changed little since. Loughborough, for example, has an apothecary, draper, innkeeper, architect, auctioneer, carpenter, hatter, farmer and grazier, Superviser of Excise, Clerk to the Magistrates, toolmaker, butcher, cutler, carrier, grocer, plumber, schoolmaster and cabinet maker.

Disasters also are often recorded on churchyard memorials, particularly in seaports and in mining areas, where catastrophe was never far away.

Making a collection of tombstone inscriptions can be a very pleasant hobby. The simplest are often the best, like the epitaph on the grave at West Pennard in Somerset of two children, both under six months, who died in 1813:

'Lifeless infants tho' we be
You may one truth from we
Think when ever you see this spot
You have sin'd but we have not.'

The country stonemason has left out 'learn' from the second line. One wonders what the parents said to him.

Chest and table tombs

Many medieval churches and cathedrals contain examples of altar tombs, a large stone chest used as the base for a recumbent effigy of the deceased. In the thirteenth century they began to appear outside the church, in the churchyard. For some time they were simply stone boxes, with no inscription and very little decoration, but in the fourteenth century the sides were carved, often to resemble church windows. Later, skulls, leaves and other forms of ornamentation were added, and the top or lid of the chest was formed by a thick stone slab, bevelled off or moulded at the edges.

In parts of the Cotswolds, you sometimes see a long, half-rounded stone running lengthways along the whole top of the tomb, with grooves cut across the stone at regular intervals. These are known as bale tombs. There are two possible explanations for the stone. Since such tombs are usually found in the woollen districts, it may possibly represent a corded bale of cloth. Another suggestion is that it shows a corpse wrapped in a woollen shroud.

Kensal Green, London

Country churchyard, circa 1850 △

Chest tombs became fairly common in the early seventeenth century and continued to be popular throughout the eighteenth. Sometimes they are of strange shapes and quite frequently they are protected by iron railings. A variant was the table tomb, in which the top was supported by legs, often elaborately carved, at each corner.

Kensal Green, London

Victorian privacy and respectability

The Victorians were strong believers in privacy, both in their homes and in their cemeteries. They refused to accept the idea that a person's bones should be moved about. A man was entitled to rest where he had been laid. To make this more likely – it could not, of course, be guaranteed – there had to be, at the very least, a large, solid headstone to mark off one burial site from another and, from the mid-nineteenth century onwards, the private plot was often outlined by a stone kerb and further protected by means of a cast-iron railing. If the railing was extended over the top, so as to form a cage, it had the extra advantage of deterring body-snatchers, in search of material to sell to medical schools.

The huge Victorian demand for monuments made it profitable for the monumental masons to sell standardized products, including railings, and to issue catalogues. Identical monuments could be seen right across the country, the more fashionable and expensive granites and Italian white marble being preferred to local materials.

Encouraged by the clergy, the same symbols of death, mourning and eternity began to appear in cemeteries everywhere – broken columns, doves, weeping classical figures, angels, urns and shells were particular favourites.

And, as with their homes, the Victorians introduced the idea which the eighteenth century would have found extraordinary, of each grave having its own private garden. For them, the cemetery was no longer a public place. It was an estate of small private dwellings.

Railed tomb, St Peter in Thanet, Kent △

36

Phiz cartoon, 1777

Symbols

The Victorians were fond of having symbols on their churchyard monuments. They used them as a religious code and knew what they meant. These are some of the most common ones:

Anchor   An early Christian symbol, meaning either hope or rest.

Bed   A deathbed. Sometimes this in turn is symbolized by a pillow.

Book   The symbol of faith. The supreme book was, of course, the Bible.

Butterfly   The Resurrection.

Column   The column is usually shown broken as an indication of mortality. Life, like the building, has lost its support.

Crown   The crown of the Christian martyr, whose reward awaits him in Heaven, after his suffering on earth.

Dove   The Holy Spirit, peace.

◁ St John's, Hampstead ▽   St Peter in Thanet, Kent ▷

Hands	Shown clasped, they symbolize farewell.	Lamp	This means either immortality, the undying flame, or the light which leads one to a knowledge of God.
Ivy	Either immortality or evergreen, undying friendship.	Laurel	Found most often on the tomb of a writer, musician or artist, the laurel signifies fame.
Lamb	This, the symbol of innocence, is found most often on children's graves.	Lion	Like the horse, a symbol of strength and courage. It can also symbolize the Resurrection.

Phoenix   The Resurrection of Christ.

Rock or   The Christian Church.
rocks

Scythe or Death. Human beings are
sickle   eventually cut down like
          ripe corn.

Shell   A pilgrimage to God or
         Heaven. The shell was the
         badge of the pilgrims who
         went to Compostella in
         Spain.

Ship   The Christian Church,
        carrying the faithful on
        their journey through life.

(*Left and above right*) Kensal Green, London

Painswick, Glos. ▽

Snake   Usually shown with its tail in its mouth, it symbolizes eternity.

Torch   If shown upright, it means immortality, but if on its side or inverted, the light of life which has been put out.

Urn   If it has flames coming from it, it signifies new life. If it is empty and draped, it means death.

Why not make a list of the symbols you find on monuments in your local churchyard or cemetery, with the dates when they were used?

Military cemeteries

The two principal military cemeteries in Britain are at Cambridge, where the American government has established its own cemetery for those of its servicemen who died in Europe during and after the Second World War, and at Aldershot, where British soldiers have been buried since the middle of last century. Both are immaculately maintained – they are certainly among the best-kept cemeteries in Britain – but, whereas the American cemetery is on flat ground and the rows and rows of regimental headstones make it somewhat monotonous, Aldershot is on hilly ground and the overall effect is that of a very pleasant park.

▽ Aldershot Military Cemetery ▷

Aldershot contains the graves of the wives and children of soldiers, as well as of soldiers themselves, so that it has much more of a family and civilian atmosphere about it than Cambridge or, for that matter, than most British military cemeteries abroad. It was established in 1856 and covers fifteen acres. Until the First World War, families were free to choose their own design of headstone. This is still permitted in the case of privately arranged burials, subject to certain regulations as to size and spacing, but official burials, that is, those paid for by the Government, have to have the standard pattern headstone, which has remained unchanged since 1918.

Aldershot Military Cemetery △

During a walk round the cemetery at Aldershot, you may be surprised at the number of foreign soldiers who are buried there, and if you look hard you may discover memorials to people of more than military importance.

43

Burial places as parks

In the course of centuries, many village churchyards, like a few fortunate ones in the centre of towns, have become little parks. There are lawns, with a few tombs and gravestones dotted about over them, and old-established trees to give shade and variety. Quite often, seats have been provided, and there are few nicer places to have your lunch on a hot day.

For one hundred and fifty years, many of the people who planned and promoted the new cemeteries spent a lot of thought and money trying to make them as green and pleasant as possible. Highgate Cemetery, in North London, had a regular staff of twenty-eight gardeners at the beginning of the present century and, among their many other duties, they raised a quarter of a million bedding-out plants each year.

But today cemetery owners can no longer afford to maintain, let alone improve and extend, such magnificent parks. The trees which exist now were nearly all planted long ago. Places like Highgate and Kensal Green may be romantic and peaceful places for a stroll, but even their greatest admirers could hardly describe them as well kept any more. Efforts are being made nowadays, however, to put things right and in some areas community volunteers are beginning to tackle the job.

St John's, Hampstead

△ Painswick, Glos., where the yew trees are particularly
fine and well cared for. In the Middle Ages parishes were
compelled to plant yews to provide wood for bows.

St Peter in Thanet, Kent ▽

The problems of neglect

Before families started to move about the country and when hand-labour was still cheap, keeping graveyards neat and tidy was no great problem. People kept the graves of their relations and ancestors free from grass and weeds as a matter of course and put fresh flowers on them from time to time, and for a very small sum an ancient man was available to keep the paths and grassy areas respectable. This is how it was until the 1920s and 1930s, when the old communities began to break up. Children left the district, aunts and uncles died, and there was nobody left to look after the family graves in the traditional way. After

the Second World War, wages began to soar and parishes and cemetery authorities could no longer afford to pay men to do the tidying-up jobs by hand. Where machinery could be used, the grass was kept mown. Where it could not, the weeds and the trees and bushes took over. Within twenty years, once immaculate graveyards turned into jungles.

Wherever possible, old headstones have been moved to the sides of the churchyard, so that the motor-mower can have a clear run. But, for most of the graves established since the middle of the nineteenth century, this was impossible, because the stone kerbs separating one grave from the next were only a foot apart. Under such circumstances it is difficult to get a pair of shears in, let alone a lawnmower. In a desperate attempt to clear the wilderness, some cemetery authorities have used herbicides and even flame-guns. Either way, the result is a burnt-up desert, which looks dreadful.

Although old cemeteries and church-yards often occupy very valuable land, it is difficult for the Church or for any other owner to sell the site, since relatives have to be traced and their permission obtained before the bones of those buried there can be moved.

It is curious to note that in village churchyards the traditional method, used for centuries, of keeping the grass trim was to graze sheep over it. One wonders why the hard-pressed owners of cemeteries have never tried the same technique.

◁ Memorial to a concert pianist, Highgate Cemetery, London

Arno's Vale cemetery, Bristol ▽

Index

Aldershot Military Cemetery, 42–3
altar tombs, 34
American cemetery, Cambridge, 42–3
animal cemeteries, 16–17
Arno's Vale cemetery, 11, 47

bale tombs, 34
Bianchi monument, 25
body-snatchers, 36–7
Burial Acts, 14

Casement mausoleum, 25
charnel houses, 19
chest tombs, 34–5
columbaria, 11
crypts, 19
cremation, 9, 10–11
Cremation Society, 10
crematoria, 10–11

death rate, 6–7
Duke of Kent, 26, 27
Duke of Wellington, 17, 20

Edinburgh, 17, 24

Frogmore, 27
funerals, 6, 7, 20

Glasgow Necropolis, 13, 14–15, 24–5
Golders Green Crematorium, 10–11
graveboards, 28

grave-lists, 22
Greyfriars Bobby, 17

Hampstead Cemetery, 25, 38, 44
headstones, 28
  cost of, 20–1
Highgate Cemetery, 9, 22–3, 44, 46

infant mortality, 5, 8, 32
inscriptions, 31–3

Kensal Green Cemetery, 13, 14, 25, 32, 33, 34, 35, 40, 41, 44
kerbs, 36, 46–7

lettering, 28–30
Liverpool Necropolis, 12, 13, 15
London Cemetery Company, 13
Loughborough churchyard, 32

Marx, Karl, 22–3
masons' catalogues, 36
mausoleums, 24–5, 27
Metropolitan Interments Act, 14
military cemeteries, 42–3
Monteath mausoleum, 24–5
monumental masons, 24, 28, 29, 36

monuments, 18, 20–1, 22–3, 24–5

neglect, 5, 22, 44, 46–7

Painswick churchyard, 21, 29, 41, 45
Père Lachaise cemetery, Paris, 13
private plots, 36
Public Health Acts, 7

railings, 36
Ricketts tomb, 25
royal family, 26–7

St George's Chapel, Windsor, 26–7
St Germain-en-Laye, 26
St Peter in Thanet, 36, 39, 45
stone, types used, 29, 36
symbols, 38–41

table tombs, 34–5
Thompson, Sir Henry, 10

Victoria, Queen, 27
Victorians, 36, 38

Westminster Abbey, 26
weathering of headstones, 28, 29
Windsor, 26–7
Woking Cemetery, 10